To: _____

From _____

thank you

so much!

Chris Shea

COUNTRYMAN

Published by J. Countryman, a division of Thomas Nelson, Inc, Nashville, Tennessee 37214.

Project manager—Terri Gibbs.

Designed by The DesignWorks Group; cover, David Uttley; interior, Robin Black. www.thedesignworksgroup.com

ISBN 1-4041-0324-4

http://www.thomasnelson.com
http://www.jcountryman.com

Printed and bound in the United States of America

To Lori and Kelly
For whom and to whom
my thanks go on forever...
and dedicated to my
dad,
Bill "Thanks" Givens...

Where do the
        unsaid thank you's
                go,

thank you's

never spoken

12

but truly,

deeply felt?

13

Thank you's for those
Christmas gifts

15

and birthday presents

16

opened long ago;

for books already read
(and thoroughly enjoyed),

candy long since eaten,

a hand-knit
sweater

worn and worn
and now outgrown,

or a day out
on the ocean

24

in a neighbor's
brand new boat.

Where could they be—

26

thank you notes for a place
    to call home for a day or
a week or two,

for borrowed cups
of sugar,

or three large eggs
for making
Pancakes,

or a bag of home-grown
oranges,

30

a gift left outside
for a Saturday surprise?

Perhaps somewhere

just out of
sight

33

these unsent
bits
of
gratitude

34

are safely

tucked

away,

just never mailed
or
said out loud,

x

37

for

reasons

now forgotten...

39

(perhaps it was
a broken
crayon,

or the perfect
phrase

42

just wouldn't
come to mind.)

or lack of proper
postage.

Me
1638 Rideout Way
Whittier DC
20071

INSUFFICIENT
POSTAGE

MOTHER & DAD
P.O. Box 19446
ANY TOWN, USA
92437

Return to
Sender

The truth about
all thank you's

46

Dear Friend,
My heart is filled
with such
gratitude at
your generosity

whether spoken or
written down,

is that they originate
within the heart
   where they stay

   permanently
         recorded,

48

timeless thoughts of
gratitude

waiting
to be said.

49

So if I've
ever failed
to say
them,

& four
profoundly
simple
words,

I'd like to say them, new,

today . . .

52

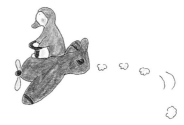

THANK YOU SO MUCH

53

Thank you for every gift
you've given
me,

54

Thank you for all the
kind things you've done,

56

and thank you most
a thousand times...

59

...just
for
being you.

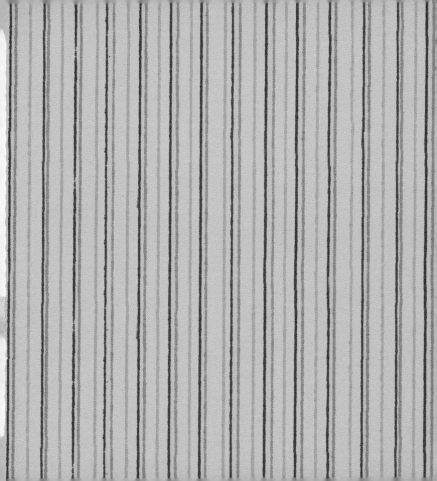